Love Letters From the Master

By: Kanisha N. Parks

Love Letters from the Master.
A collection of inspirational Christian poetry.

ISBN: 1448693950
EAN-13: 9781448693955

Copyright © 2009 Kanisha N. Parks

All Rights Reserved. This book may not be reproduced, scanned, or distributed in any printed or electronic form without the express written permission of the author. Please do not participate in or encourage piracy of copyrighted materials in violation of the author's rights.

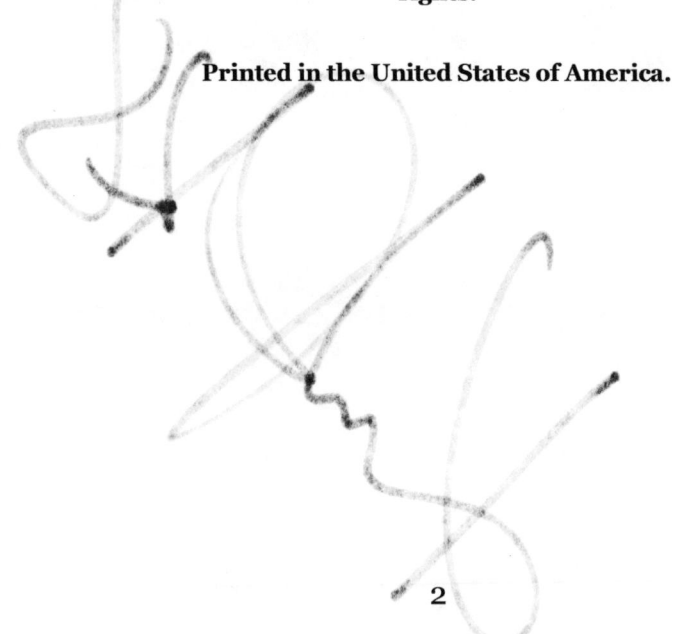

Printed in the United States of America.

**Thank You, God for blessing me with this amazing gift.
I live to be used by You.**

table of contents.

Devotion:

A Reason to Praise	7-8
As I Am	9-10
Brand New	11-12
Can I Be Closer to You?	13-14
I'm A Changed Person	15-16
I'm Comin' Home	17-18
Available	19-20
Love Poem	21-22
Speechless	23-24
When I Fell in Love with Jesus	25-26
When I Think of the Lord	27-28
Work on Me	29-30
Your Love Works Miracles	31-32
You're Everything	33-34
You're Welcome	35-36
Yours Truly	37-38
Blessed	39-40
He Reigns	41-42
In Control	43-44
Make Time for Me	45-46

Encouragement:

As Long As	49-50
Christian Soldiers	51-52
Define Yourself	53-54
Forgiveness Prayer	55-55
Give it all to God in Prayer	57-58
God's Got It	59-60
God's Healing Power	61-62
He is There	63-64
I Am	65-66
I Desire	67-68
I Go to Him	69-70
I Know Who I Am in Christ	71-72
Let Him Be Your Everything	73-74
My God Can	75-76
Never Be the Same	77-78
No More	79-80
On My Knees	81-82
Pressing On	83-84
Too Far to Turn Back Now	85-86
We are Blessed	87-88
When All Else Fails	89-90
When We Get to Heaven	91-92
You Decide	93-94

Devotion

"I will sing to the LORD all my life;
I will sing praise to my God as long as I live."
-Psalm 104:33

A Reason to Praise

I have a reason to praise,
For God has never forsaken me.
My heart is overcome with joy.
My tongue shall continually exalt Thee.

I cannot keep my mouth shut
Because God has done too many great things.
He wants and deserves the glory He is due.
Let Him be praised by every human being.

Sometimes my journey gets a little hard,
And sometimes it gets a little tough.
But I cannot just sit here as if He's not worthy,
When the breath in my body is proof enough.

Yes, I have fallen short of His glory,
And yes, I have done wrong.
But my God has forgiven me,
And that is why I can sing my song.

Whenever I come to church,
My hands shall be raised.
Because I have breath in my body,
I have a reason to praise.

As I Am

Broken, torn,
Defeated, and bound.
These barriers in front of me,
And I can't see any way out.

Scars of the past,
Constantly remind me of my sins.
Where does the pain end
And healing begin?

I try to get up, but yet
I stumble, and fall.
Don't know how up feels,
'Cause I been down through it all.

"Tell me why!" you call,
And hope against hope that an answer is near.
And one day, I heard it,
Ever so softly in my ear,

"Come to me, as you are,"
He called.
And the answer was so simple,
All I could do was fall.

Fall, that is, into the arms
Of God, who was always there.
God, who never ceases to forgive,
Never ceases to care.

Don't worry about the scars,
And forget about your pain.
Come to Him as you are,
And He'll erase the stains.

I don't need to come to God,
In glitz and in glam,
Because He opens his arms to me,
Just as I am.

Brand New

Brand New.
That is what I consider myself to be
Because God has taken over,
And has done a total change in me.

I haven't been made over,
But instead I'm a completely new creature.
Reflecting God's ways and His attributes,
In my every feature.

Now He's my all in all,
My way out of no way,
And He supplies my needs,
Day after day.

I have no need to fret,
Be weary, or worry.
Because now I'm doing His will,
Steadfast and in a hurry.

I desire to be in His presence,
To worship Him for all He's done,
Knowing that from now on in my life,
God will always be number one.

I have a heart after Him,
Because He gave His love to me.
So I don't set my own goals,
But I'll be whatever He wants me to be.

Look at the new me,
Doing what God wants me to do.
Because now I'm in His will and His plan.
I've been made Brand New.

Can I Be Closer to You?

Can I be closer to You, God?
For that's all I desire to be.
Can you get rid of the old,
And do a new thing in me?

The thoughts I have thought, Lord,
They don't line up with Your will.
So give me a new mind,
Where Your Word is instilled.

I've been on an emotional roller coaster,
So give me a heart just like yours.
This time only You will dwell there,
So that I can love you more.

Whatever You want me to do,
I just want to serve You.
I will kill this flesh no matter what.
I will do what you say do.

Can I be closer to you, God?
Can you show me your ways?
Can I walk, talk, and be just like You
For all the rest of my days?

Now that I'm cleansed from sin,
Anointed fresh, and anointed new,
Lord, this day, I'm simply asking,
Can I be closer to You?

I'm A Changed Person

I'm a changed person,
Because I don't do the things I used to.
I've stopped doing what I want to do,
And I've started following You.

I'm a changed person,
Because I am following where you lead me.
Forgetting about my plans for my life,
And being what You want me to be.

I've forgotten the old,
And I now look forward to the new.
With each day and every step,
I make sure I'm following You.

Your hand is where my heart belongs,
This one thing I know.
I'm not staying stuck in the same place anymore,
It's time for me to grow.

I have no need to return,
To the former things I have done.
Because I'm following you and Your will,
So I know that victory is won.

I keep you first in my life,
And I'll never let another take your place.
For it is only by you and your mercy,
That all of my sins are erased.

I'm a changed person,
Because I don't do what I used to.
I've stopped doing what I want to do,
And now I'm following You.

I'm Comin' Home

I'm comin' back home,
Back to safety, love, and care.
In the shelter of the Most High,
Who saves me from the fowler's snare.

I have rebelled against my daddy's ways,
Thinking I could make it on my own.
But I was wrong to think these things,
So now I'm comin' home.

Back to the shadow of the Almighty,
Where no harm can come upon me.
For my daddy has said,
"My angels shall guard Thee".

But I'm not coming back home,
With my dirty hands,
But I'll cleanse myself from all my sins,
And Follow God's commands.

I will now draw nigh to Him,
So He can draw nigh to me.
Doing exactly what He wants me to do,
And being who He wants me to be.

I'm going to purify my heart,
And let go of my double-minded ways.
I will humble myself before Him,
And do all that He says.

I'm tired of being a sinner,
And I'm tired of being so alone.
So I'm giving up life as I know it,
And I'm comin' back home.

Available

I avail my mind unto you, Lord.
That I shall have a mind like Christ.
Fill it with thoughts of love, kindness, and humility.
Instead of hatred, envy and strife.

I avail my hands unto you, Lord
That I shall perform the works your will requires.
May anointing flow from them for your kingdom
And not my own selfish desires.

I avail my feet unto you, Lord.
That they'll only go where you send
They are for your use always, Lord
And are not mine to lend.

I avail my heart unto you, Lord.
So that I can trust you with it all.
I'm yours for all of eternity, Lord-
There whenever you call.

I avail my body unto you, Lord.
Help me keep this temple holy every day.
Even as a living sacrifice I know
I couldn't compare to the price Jesus paid.

I am available unto you, Lord
In every way I can possibly be.
Thank you for everything you are, Lord.
Thank you for using me.

Love Poem

In awe.
That's the only way to describe how I feel right now.
The way that you love me and the things that you do—I could never know why or how.

I look around this world and see
All the amazing things you have done.
As you make and mold me
I realize this journey's just begun.

The way that you love us
There is no one else who can
Teach the mother to be a better woman,
The father to be a better man.

When we worship you in the spirit
And we pour out to you,
It's not because we want anything
It's just because it's due.

Every time I'm in your Presence
I leave wanting more.
You're changing me so powerfully,
I'll never be what I was before.

You lead me through the fire
And hold my hand in the rain.
You loved me through my sorrow
And you erased the pain.

I just want you to know
I love and adore you more than anything
When people told me I couldn't fly
You're the one gave me wings.

Through the words of this poem
I hope you accept my worship up above
You've given me the best gift of all-
You've shown me how to love.

Speechless

I awaken to the blissfulness of your Presence
And open my heart.
So tenderly does your love fill me,
Giving my day a peaceful start.

The awesomeness of your Glory
Makes me thirst after you.
And just to be in the midst of your majesty
Is all I want to do.

To share the joy of your Presence
Is my ultimate desire
That others will search for you
To also take them higher.

My relationship with you
Is the water that keeps me spiritually alive
Without your love and devotion to me
I could never survive.

I long for you like a drought
Does for the rain
Always needing and yearning for you
That precious time with you again.

Being in his holy of holies
Is an experience I can't fully describe
All I know is
It's the best medicine I could ever prescribe

Thank you God for who you are
And what you do for me
Your love takes my very breath away
And leaves me without speech.

When I Fell in Love With Jesus

When I fell in love with Jesus,
My life was totally changed.
I don't feel hurt anymore.
But I feel completely rearranged.

He took every broken piece,
And He put it right back together.
I can't help but praise His name.
I will worship Him forever.

All the past disappointments,
I no longer have to care.
Because He took away the heavy burden,
That I used to bear.

I now keep away from all the things,
That held me down before.
As for all of those things,
I will not do them anymore.

My eyes have opened up,
And it's very plain for me to see,
That the Devil himself,
Has nothing good in store for me.

God polished this heart of mine,
And now it shines just like gold.
Because of all He has done for me,
My testimony will be told.

I've got something to shout about,
And I'm telling you, Lord, I will.
All those times I abandoned you,
And yet you loved me still.

When I fell in love with Jesus,
My life was totally changed.
I don't feel hurt anymore.
But I feel completely rearranged.

When I Think of the Lord

When I start to think of the Lord,
So much happiness begins to fill me.
I forget about all of the negativity around,
And how great You are is all I see.

I think of how great it'll be,
When I can finally be with you in the sky.
I imagine how I will worship you,
Oh, God, who reigns on high.

I want to love you even more,
Because you'll never hurt me, like others do.
And when I'm lonely and in need of comfort,
I know I can turn to you.

When I think of the Lord,
I think of the love He has for everyone,
How he cared so much for us,
To send His only begotten son.

I think of His angels
And the love they have for us, too.
For God has appointed two to me,
And two for each and every one of you.

When I begin to think of the Lord,
Sorrow instantly leaves me.
I forget about all of the negativity around me,
And how great You are is all I see.

Work on Me

Chisel me up or cut away.
Remove something and then re-do.
Whatever it takes for you to work,
Lord I'm giving it all to you.

As you begin to shape and build,
Making me into what you called me to be,
I'm moving myself out of the way,
So you can build this church in me.

It's not going to be easy—
That's one thing that I'm sure of.
But God, I'm in this for the long haul,
And until You're done, I won't give up.

Change me, break me,
Make me, mold me, and build.
As you work on me, lord,
Unto you I yield.

Surrendering unto you my life,
My purpose, my all.
Because you became first in my life,
The day that you called.

Called me back home,
And out of my sinful state,
And once I surrendered,
You began to create.

And ever since that day,
I look around and see,
I'm not that person anymore.
I've let the past go, God—

So work on me.

Your Love Works Miracles

God, your love works miracles,
In people's lives every day.
Shaping, making, molding,
And changing in every way.

Sitting on the ground of my heart,
And spiritually feeding me.
Showing me how this Godly love,
Is truly meant to be.

This love is not magical,
Like a made-up Fairyland.
But it something real.
Something much more grand.

It's a love that captures my heart,
And holds me in the midnight hour.
No love can work miracles like this.
No love holds this love's power.

This love reassures me,
That God is always there.
That He will never leave me.
For His love is in the midst of the air.

God, your love works miracles,
In people's lives everyday.
Shape me, make me, mold me,
And change me in every way.

You're Everything

Who is the One,
Who created the earth and every human being?
It is the Lord, who sits on High,
For He is everything.

Love is who you are.
No greater love is there than yours.
When sorrow fills our hearts,
Down from heaven your love pours.

The Greatest Friend is who you are.
For you listen to each word we say.
Friends on earth may someday fade away,
But your friendship is here to stay.

The Savior is who you are.
For you sent your Son to die for our sins.
He gave His life for us all,
So that we may live again.

A shield is who you are,
Forever protecting us from all evil things.
We will never have to worry as long as we have you,
For we are children of the King.

God is who you are.
No other word can say it best.
Lord, Jehovah, Emmanuel,
And all the rest.

You are all powerful.
And You are all-seeing,
If nothing else,
You are everything.

You're Welcome

I welcome you into this room Lord,
I welcome you to have your way.
I welcome you to lead and direct my path-
What I should and shouldn't I say.

I want you to show me
All the marvelous things you can do.
With my entire life, Lord.
I am entrusting you.

I'm completely and utterly amazed
By how your love has blessed me.
I haven't been the same since you touched me
And set my soul free

You Lord are welcome into my heart,
Where I desire for only you to reside.
To you I can run in times of utter sorrow.
In you I shall confide.

You're welcome into my home, Lord
Please bless every room with your presence.
When trials and tribulations come I won't worry-
But just fall to my knees and give you reverence.

Take control of my life's purpose, Lord
Otherwise I won't know what to do.
I put aside my own will and way
And Lord, I welcome you.

Yours Truly

I give you myself
and everything that it entails
I want You to use me
so Your glory will be unveiled

Show me how to trust you
as we walk hand in hand
Teach me how to do all
that I can to stand

Allow me to walk upright
and follow in Your way.
Bless my tongue to speak Your words
May I quietly obey.

I know that You will never leave me
So I'm confident in Your Word.
Break up the pride in me
Heal the pain and the hurt

I want to be close to You
Please draw nigh unto me
Anoint my hands again
Anoint mine eyes to see

I love you forever
Let your light shine through me
I'm staying in Your will, Lord
I am Yours Truly.

Blessed

When I look around at all the amazing things You've done,
I know that I cannot complain.
Instead I stand in awe of you,
And I begin to praise Your name.

When man said I'd never make it,
You showed me that I could.
When I myself doubted if I'd perform Your works
You showed me that I would.

You anointed these hands
So I give them back to You.
I'm so blessed to have this gift,
So blessed to be used by You.

I don't question my purpose
Instead I'll just do what you say.
I trust you Lord with everything that I have
I will seek you for the way.

No matter what it takes
I'll follow you anyhow.
No more putting this off for later
I've got to serve you now.

I love you with all of my heart
May no one else dwell there but You.
I am who you called me to be,
I'm part of the chosen few.

You have blessed me
So that others can be blessed, too.
I'm not living for selfish gain
I'm living to be used by You.

He Reigns

The beauty of Your holiness
Envelops the atmosphere.
Your presence is just as welcome in my heart
As it is in here.

I could search the high seas
And the oceans blue
But I'd never find anyone greater
For all of creation leads me back to you.

Your sovereignty is realer to me
Than even the things I can touch and see.
I'm amazed by Your works of art,
How you fearfully and wonderfully made me.

Every knee shall bow
And every tongue shall confess.
To give you reverence, Lord,
For you deserve nonetheless.

Everything that you've given me
I live to give back to You.
I want you to ignite me with Your spirit
So that a reinvention may ensue.
I am yours forever,
Just as you gave Your only begotten son for me.
In You I've found who I am,
And everything I ever want to be.

You are the essence of holiness,
And we worship Your name.
He is Lord of all,
And forever, He reigns.

In Control

I've given my life
Completely over to You.
This faith walk to me
Is absolutely new.

I'm learning to trust You
With everything that I am.
I'm learning to obey
As I listen to your master plan.

My ears are wide open,
Even though I may feel blind.
I know that I'm not lost
Because you speak to my mind.

I don't have to worry
Because you already know.
I'll stay in my seat of waiting.
Until the plan is shown.

I used to try and do everything
All on my own.
But since I gave it all to you
I've mentally and spiritually grown.
It's amazing how much we try to fight against your will
When all you want us to do is trust you—
And on your word stand still.

For you are in control, Lord.
I'm seeking only Your plan.
You made me a new creature—
My life is in Your hands.

Make Time for Me

We're always too busy
Or too preoccupied for God to use.
Even when it comes down to the small things,
We're quick to supply an excuse.

Finding reasons to slack on your duties
And shirk out on what you should do,
In order to take the chance to do things
That only seem to belittle you.

It's funny how we make time for things
That don't matter over the ones that should indeed.
We rush to do the things that we want,
Instead of making an effort to do the ones we need.

But God is beckoning for someone
Who'll give Him their heart, mind, and soul.
Someone who'll sacrifice their own wishes,
And allow God to begin to mold.

He needs someone who is willing to say:
"Use me, Lord, I'm yours."
Someone who's willing to kill the flesh
And give unto God all the more.

Someone who if time doesn't avail itself
Will find a way to make some.
Someone striving to move forward in God,
Letting go of where they've come from.

So when it comes down to it;
It's about sifting out what's important to us.
And when it comes down to the Lord,
Making time for Him is a must.

Encouragement
"Therefore encourage one another and build each other up, just as in fact you are doing."
-1 Thessalonians 5:11

As Long As

As long as the wind blows,
And we have air to breathe.
As long as the sun still shines
And the beautiful days never leave.

As long as the ones that we love
Are safe, sound, and near,
And we have the ability to pay our bills
When they get here.

As long as the boss acts right
And nothing in our life is grim.
You see, it's easy for us
To be able to trust Him.

But what if the sun stopped shining
And our bills weren't paid
What if He didn't wake you up on time,
And you ended up being late?

What if those you love turn on you
And your life is no longer bliss?
Does the God He's always been,
Suddenly cease to exist?

No! Because even in the rain,
And the dark seasons that pass,
God is still God,
And His love is what will last.

When you don't know where or how
You'll get the money for the bills,
And you don't know how to pay
For your family's next meal.

Turn to the God He's always been,
And this, too, will pass.
Then you'll really know if you can trust Him,
More than just "as long as".

Christian Soldiers

Keeping God first in our life
Is something we often forget to do.
In the midst of our hectic days, God,
we always seem too busy for you.

So hard it is to find the time
To meditate and pray.
So easy is it to protest
Instead of quietly obey.

But God wants someone who's tired of making excuses
and is ready to execute His will.
Someone to take up their cross and follow Him;
To on His word stand still.

Oh the time we waste
Trying to do the things we desire.
God wants a willing soldier
Who'll forsake mediocre in order to go higher.

This walk is not easy
Nor for the faint of heart.
And if you don't plan to see it through until the end
Then you shouldn't even attempt to start.

For many are called
But God has chosen a select few—
Those who have their mind made up
And are ready for the work they must do.

It does get tough but we walk by faith
And not by sight.
Satan desires to sift us as wheat,
So we must always be prepared for this Christian fight.

Define Yourself

Bold, beautiful, loud and strong.
That's how I define me.
Despite what others think,
Or the fact that they may disagree.

I stand ever so firmly on the truth,
That I am exactly who I say I am.
And if I believe I can do something,
There's no one who can tell me that I can't.

My past doesn't define who I am.
Because God has forgiven me of it all.
I move forward, not letting anyone stop me
From moving on, and standing tall.

As far as the east is from the west,
Is how far He has placed my sins from me.
So, now, when I look in the mirror,
That old person is not who I see.

I see a whole new creature,
Who isn't bound by yester-years.
Because He has deleted the pain and the shame
So I no longer have to fear.

Fear being what He called me to be,
Or trusting Him when I don't see the way.
Fear that I'll never come out of darkness,
And step into my brighter day.

Because now I have.
And only I can define K-a-n-i-s-h-a.
Let the past go,
Define yourself today.

Forgiveness Prayer

I come to you, Father,
On my knees, in order to pray.
Asking you for forgiveness,
Of my sins this day.

I know I'm not worthy,
Of the love that You give,
But I thank You for dying on the cross,
So that I might live.

I'm tired of living in sin,
And doing the things I do,
So deliver me, set me free,
So I can be more pleasing to you.

Jesus, I thank you,
For shedding your blood for me.
For taking the guilt of my sins,
So I might be free.

I haven't always done,
What I know I should do,
But please receive me back,
So I can do goodness in the sight of you.

Cleanse me, Oh Father,
Of all of my sin.
Make me into a better person,
So I can be clean within.

I want to be used,
For your glory divine,
So forgive me now, oh Father,
So that this chance may be mine.

I thank you, God,
For forgiving, and forgetting my sins,
So that I may be pleasing to you,
As well as clean within.

Give it all to God in Prayer

Give it all to God in prayer,
Let Him turn it all around for you.
Stop trying to fix what you cannot,
And let Him do what He needs to do.

Give God every trouble,
That you have been unfortunate to see.
Because He's the only one you need.
Take it from me.

I turned to everything and everyone,
Seeking answers in all the wrong places.
But only My Father in Heaven knew how to help.
I should have sought only His face.

Know this, I must now tell you.
There is no need to fret, and no need to cry.
Your God in Heaven will meet all your needs,
And He is more than able to supply.

Whatever you may be going through,
The answer is surely not in man.
Let God give you the answers you need,
Because only He can.

No more going around the mulberry bush,
Blindly seeking answers from whomever you come to.
Because only God can bring peace to the situation.
Let Him reach down and comfort you.

Give it all to God in Prayer.
Let Him turn it all around for you.
Stop trying to fix what you cannot,
And let the Lord do what He needs to do.

God's Got It

Searching for answers, wants, and necessities
in man
Is a quest you'll surely fail to fulfill.
Trying so hard to run from the Father,
When your success is in His perfect will.

Asking questions like,
"Who, what, when, where, and why?"
When all you really need to do
Is give God a try.

You'll never fill the void in your heart,
By allowing others to come inside.
Pretend you're happy as can be,
But from God you can never hide.

Because God's got it—
Everything you'll ever need and more.
Just let go of all the mess you're holding on
to—What are you waiting for?

Out of all He's done and all He does,
Waking you up day after day,
Not to mention his brand new mercies,
Or the price He sent His son to pay.

God's got much better in store for you,
Than what you've experienced up until this time.
Accept His call upon your life;
No greater love will you ever find.

No matter who you are,
God is the perfect fit.
Your needs, wants, and then some—
Just know that God's got it.

God's Healing Power

I know miracles are real,
And God's power is, too.
I know God is amazing,
And I know He can heal you.

Because He has healed you,
Many, many times before.
In all of God's excellency,
I know He can heal you even more.

God has so many plans,
That only you can fulfill.
To tell of God's goodness,
You can, and you will.

You are God's passion.
You're His jewel of gold.
What you're going through now,
Is just another testimony to be told.

So keep your faith,
Every day, and every hour.
Just watch, and you'll see,
God's healing power.

Dedicated to My Grandmother, Fannie Burton

He Is There

When times get hard,
And you feel you cannot maintain,
Most people don't think to get on their knees,
And call upon God's holy name.

As time passes by,
Our burdens seem to become harder to bear.
We turn to our friends for help,
But it seems that no one is there.

So instead we don't ask for assistance,
And fight our battles all alone.
With our heads hung and filled with pity,
We mumble and we groan.

But one day, there'll come a time,
When you do away with your stubborn pride,
Because God will open your eyes,
And how much you really need Him, you'll realize.

He is there to ease the pain.
He is there to dry the tears
He is there to answer your questions
And He is there to calm your fears.

He'll shed light on your dark situation,
And cause your cloudy days to disappear.
And when you're feeling all by yourself,
You can rest assured that God is near.

Because He is there when think you don't need Him,
And He is there when you know you do.
He's always just one prayer away,
And close enough to rescue you.

I Am

I am who God says I am,
For by His grace I've been changed.
Walking upright in His light,
And blessing His holy name.

I am a Child of the Most High God,
Forever following the King.
For it is He who has saved me,
And given me my being.

I am a New Creature,
Putting the old behind me,
I'm reaching forward in my life,
Being who God wants me to be.

I am a living testimony of God,
And all that He can surely do.
Showing others how my God,
Can change something old into something new.

I am the Branch,
While Jesus is the True Vine.
Remaining in His will while He has His way,
So the blessing can be mine.

I am a vessel of love,
For God has first loved me.
Allowing my love and my joy,
To open someone else's eyes to see.

I am who God says I am,
For by His grace I've been changed.
Walking upright in His light,
And blessing His holy name.

I Desire

Worldly possessions will pile up,
And mount to nothing at all.
So what do you do when your world
Seems to crumble, and fall?

This desire within the depths of my soul
Beckons for something more.
Ever so blindly, I search for answers,
Never finding what I'm looking for.

Then you reach down from heaven,
And open my eyes.
And I am now aware of where
My true desire lies.

My desire is for Christ,
The only one who can fill this void in my soul
My desire is for Christ,
The only one who can make me completely whole.

I can't find this in anyone else,
And trust me; neither will you.
So stop trying to isolate yourself from Him
And receive what He's calling you to.

That is, a better life,
A call to something higher.
You may not realize it,
But God is your deepest desire.

I Go to Him

For my wants, needs, desires,
And all of the above,
I go to the Father—
I thirst for His love.

I look for His approval
In everything that I do.
Because His opinion matters, not man's—
In whatever I put my hands to.

He's my best friend,
And I find comfort in His presence.
I live, breathe, and exist to praise His name
And give Him reverence.

I want the words of my mouth and the
Meditation of my heart to be acceptable in
His sight.
When I feel lost in this world I remember
He is the way, the truth, and the life.

I'm never alone
Because He'll never leave nor forsake me.
In His will lies everything that I'll ever want,
And everything I'll ever need.

I'm so delighted to know Him
The way that I do.
I wish that everyone on Earth
Would have a desire to know Him too.

I Know Who I Am in Christ

I know who I am in Christ,
So the enemy has no authority over me.
And no longer will He dissuade me,
From being who God wants me to be.

I know my God has anointed me,
So go ahead and say what you will,
Talk bad about me, just making me stronger.
I'll be what God called me to be still.

I'm on a mandate to win souls for Christ,
And nothing will take away my drive.
I'm going to keep moving higher to new levels in God,
And Satan won't stop this strive.

Only I have the authority to talk about me.
So just try it, if you dare.
For 'vengeance is mine', saith the Lord,
And I have no reason to care.

I boast in my God,
Because of Him I am so proud.
I will tell of His goodness upon the mountaintops,
And sing His name out loud.

I'm a child of the Most High God,
Who only thinks good thoughts towards me,
And He has called me into greatness.
I'm going to be all He called me to be.

Let Him Be Your Everything

Let the Lord be your everything,
The one and only one in your heart.
Let Him love and care for you,
And from Him, never depart.

Put all your devotion into Him,
And dedicate your life to His plan.
Let Him shape and mold you,
Loving you like no one else can.

Let Him give you a peace,
That could only come from Heaven above,
And remove all the hurt and pain,
By just showing you His unconditional love.

Get caught up in His presence,
Forgetting about the cares of tomorrow.
Allow His joy to fill you,
And let go of all your sorrows.

Put your total trust in Him,
And you'll realize He'll always be there.
You will never have to worry about a thing,
As long as you're in His care.

Let the Lord be your everything,
For He'll wash away all of your sins.
Let Him love and care for you,
And you'll never have to search again.

My God Can

Do you serve a god,
Who can do what my God can do?
My God is powerful and mighty,
For He created both me and you.

My God can create a clean heart in you,
And renew your mind.
A love like my God gives,
In man you'll never be able to find.

My God can use one man's rib,
And create a whole new creature.
For my God created you and me,
Down to our very last feature.

My God can move mountains,
And cause the whole earth to be still.
My God can cleanse you from all impurities,
And with righteousness, refill.

My God can look past all your faults,
And every need, He will surely meet.
My God wins at all He does,
And never sees defeat.

My God can make something out of nothing,
And put the devil to shame.
My God can change your life for the better.
So you'll never be the same.

Do you serve a god,
Who can do what my God can do?
If not, accept Him into your life.
He'll do great and mighty things for you, too.

Never Be the Same

Ever since I came into Christ,
I have been a new creature.
God got rid of my tarnished qualities,
And gave me new features.

Now my walk is different,
And my talk is brand new.
I'm not an open vessel for the enemy,
But I'm open only to God's use.

To bless so many others,
And draw them all to Christ
To help them see there is a better way,
By setting an example with my life.

The things of the past are no more
Because my life has been redeemed.
The devil thought he had me,
But things aren't always what they seem.

God gave me the victory,
By using me when I felt I had defeat.
He proved to me that I am strong,
Though the enemy told me I was weak.

He raised me up from the grave
That I put myself in.
He removed all of the chains,
And released me from the sin.

But none of this would've happened
If I'd never called upon Jesus' name.
If you call on Him, He'll do it for you, too,
And trust me—you'll never be the same.

No More

No more pain, no more shame,
No more nights full of tears.
No more shackles, no more bondage.
No more hopelessness and fear.

No more insecurities,
No more never-ending lies.
No more searching for love,
And only ending up with fruitless tries.

See, in Christ,
The pasts we have are taken away.
And we become new creatures,
With a clean slate.

Haven't you had enough?
Of all the sleepless nights?
Just searching for a way out,
When there is none in sight?

His name is Jesus—
The Lover of my Soul.
He will never cause us any pain,
Our very hearts He holds.

Release the past,
Release the pain.
Open up unto the joy He brings,
And you'll never be the same.

I want to be closer to you,
I want to know the essence of who you are.
Move forward in God with me,
And leave your sins afar.

To hold on to all that pain and agony,
There is no reason for.
Decide that you're letting it all go.
Finally, you can say, "No More".

On My Knees

Whenever I'm bombarding Heaven,
On my knees seeking His holy face,
I completely tune into Him and Him only.
All other thoughts are erased.

I spend precious time with Him,
And we simply communicate.
All the love and adoration He has for me,
I more than appreciate.

I cry out to Him,
And He hears me, casting out all my fear.
I can feel His loving arms wrapped around me.
And I know my God is near.

Through every word I cry out to Him with,
He draws nearer and nearer.
He opens my eyes to see the way He's making,
And the path becomes clearer.

The greatness of His love is revealed unto me,
And my joy begins to overflow.
What people say matters no more,
What God thinks of me is all I know.

If you ever have a problem,
And you need to be set free,
Don't look to anyone else but God.
The answer's in prayer on your knees.

Pressing On

It's hard to hold on,
When everything is pressing against you.
It seems your circumstance is the same,
Nothing's changed, nothing's new.

Your past comes to haunt you,
And shame engulfs your mind.
You're spending more time with your tears
Than in prayer, you've come to find.

Now life as you know it is shattered,
And God is nowhere to be found.
When really, it's you who's been gone--
God has always been around.

Someone needs to take their life back,
And stop letting Satan get the upper hand.
Realize that your freedom won't come
automatically
It's something you must demand.

Press on, my sister, my brother,
And my friend.
Keep waiting on the Lord,
Until you've reached the end.

Look towards your future,
Because God brought you out of your past.
The Lord has made you first,
When you used to be last.

Too Far to Turn Back Now

The swampland of life before Christ
Seems to reach out to us every day-
Tempting us to go back to the messes we were before,
And turn from the Lord's way.

The sin looks so enticing,
It's a fight to force your feet to go straight ahead.
So hard it seems just to stand,
And not follow Satan instead.

But great for those who hold on,
Is the reward they shall receive.
So in the end, it's better to stand the trials,
Than it is to just pack up and leave.

Because He said He'll never put more on you,
Than He knows you can bear.
So try, hard as it may be, to remember that—
Even when life seems so unfair.

When your back's against the wall,
And all hope seems to be lost,
Are you willing to forget all that,
And trust God, whatever the cost?

It's better to focus on what God is doing,
Than the things you may lack.
Look forward in Him, keep your eyes on the prize,
And don't ever look back.

We Are Blessed

I realize that I am so blessed,
When I think of all the things God has done for me.
Because He alone has blessed me with so many things,
And brought me from where I used to be.

How many times do we become vexed in life,
Because of the things we have not yet received,
When we could be busying ourselves,
Praying for those who don't in Christ believe?

And how many times have we idolized,
Those who are famous and wealthy,
When we could be bombarding Heaven,
For those who are dying and unhealthy?

I wonder if we focused more of our energy,
On those less fortunate than we may be,
How many people would put their trust in God,
And be able to be set free.

We are truly blessed,
Even thought we don't yet have some things we'd like to
Fret not over the things you don't yet have,
But think of all He's already done for you.

God has done so much for me,
And I know I have no reason to be stressed.
Maybe we don't have everything we want,
But I still know that we are blessed.

When All Else Fails

When all else fails,
Believe In Jesus Christ.
He will never leave nor forsake you,
And He knows what's right.

When things come against you,
Have absolutely no fear.
Late in the midnight hour,
God is still safely near.

When all else fails,
Give your problems to Jesus Christ.
He won't abandon you,
And He'll work miracles in your life.

Count on Him, and trust in Him alone,
For He always knows what to do.
He can handle your situation.
He'll do it just for you.

He'll dry all of your tears,
And He'll heal your soul.
After He does all these things,
Your testimony must be told.

In Jesus Christ,
Evil cannot prevail.
In the end, you'll realize He was there all along
When all else fails.

When We Get to Heaven

Have you ever stopped to think,
Of how wonderful life will be,
When we get to Heaven with the Lord,
Our Savior, Father, and King?

Well, I have taken the time to imagine,
How marvelous it will be on that day.
I wonder if I'll be speechless,
Or have so many things to say.

Just the thought of seeing Jesus and God,
And the mansion He's preparing for me in the sky.
I wonder if I'll jump up and down,
Or fall onto my knees and cry.

But one thing that I know for sure,
Is that I shall rejoice.
No sorrow will ever fill me again.
I will praise Him and raise my voice.

That one special day keeps me motivated.
Because I will hear Him say, "Well done."
And then I will praise my Lord, my King.
Because the victory has been won.

When we get to heaven, won't we have a good time?
How we will dance, and how we will sing.
When we all get to Heaven with the Lord,
Our Savior, Father, and King.

You Decide

Whether today will be good or bad
Is your choice
What everybody else thinks subsides
To only your voice

You decide how you'll live your life:
Pleasing to God or to your flesh.
To listen to Satan's foolishness,
Or to turn to God for what's best.

Not to say that it'll be easy
To follow the Lord's way,
But the reward for doing so
Is better than man could ever pay.

This flesh is so fickle,
We all know that it's true,
But God knows you better than you know yourself
So why listen to you?

It's amazing the things you will obtain
When you decide to follow Christ
Stop trying to deck it out on your own
And trust Him with your life.

You decide—
Good day or bad, His will or yours?
You'll soon find God's way
Is the right course.

You're Beautiful

How many times have you looked in the mirror
And not liked what you see?
Well instead look inside that mirror and say,
"I love me."

Pray and ask God to show you
What He finds in you.
He'll touch your eyes
And help you to be able to see it too.

While you are praying,
Take back control of your mind
Once you achieve that,
Everything else will fall in line.

You won't look at yourself
And try to point out every flaw,
Instead of pointing out what you disliked
You'll thank God for it all.

It used to be that seeing yourself in God's eyes
And not man's was always hard
But now you'll step out in confidence-
You know who you are.

You are a child of the most High God
Who deserves nothing less than the best
Put everything you have in God's hands-
He'll handle the rest.

So when you look in that mirror,
Beautiful is all you should see.
No more feeling depressed about yourself—
Because God has set you free.

Made in the USA